DONNA WALKER TILESTON

What Every Teacher Should Know About
Classroom Management and Discipline

W0008375

CORWIN PRESS
A Sage Publications Company
Thousand Oaks, California

For information:

Corwin Press
A Sage Publications Company
2455 Teller Road
Thousand Oaks, California 91320
www.corwinpress.com

Sage Publications Ltd.
6 Bonhill Street
London EC2A 4PU
United Kingdom

Sage Publications India Pvt. Ltd.
B-42, Panchsheel Enclave
Post Box 4109
New Delhi 110 017 India

Printed in the United States of America

Library of Congress Cataloging-in-Publication Data

Tileston, Donna Walker.
What every teacher should know about classroom
management and discipline / Donna Walker Tileston.
      p. cm. — (What every teacher should know about; v.6)
Includes bibliographical references and index.
ISBN 0-7619-3122-8 (Paper)
   1. Classroom management. 2. Discipline. I. Title II. Series.
LB3013.T53 2003
371.102´4—dc21   2003010239

This book is printed on acid-free paper.

        04   05   06   10   9   8   7   6   5   4   3

Acquisitions Editor:	Faye Zucker
Editorial Assistant:	Stacy Wagner
Production Editor:	Diane S. Foster
Copy Editor:	Kris Bergstad
Typesetter:	C&M Digitals (P) Ltd.
Proofreader:	Mary Meagher
Indexer:	Molly Hall
Cover Designer:	Tracy E. Miller
Production Artist:	Lisa Miller

Contents

About the Author

Donna Walker Tileston, Ed.D., is a veteran teacher of 27 years and the president of Strategic Teaching and Learning, a consulting firm that provides services to schools throughout the United States and Canada. Also an author, Donna's publications include *Strategies for Teaching Differently: On the Block or Not* (Corwin Press, 1998), *Innovative Strategies of the Block Schedule* (Bureau of Education and Research [BER], 1999), and *Ten Best Teaching Practices: How Brain Research, Learning Styles, and Standards Define Teaching Competencies* (Corwin Press, 2000), which has been on Corwin's best-seller list since its first year in print.

Donna received her B.A. from the University of North Texas, her M.A. from East Texas State University, and her Ed.D. from Texas A & M University-Commerce. She may be reached at www.strategicteachinglearning.com or by e-mail at dwtileston@yahoo.com.

Acknowledgments

My sincere thanks go to my Acquisitions Editor, Faye Zucker, for her faith in education and what this information can do to help all children be successful. Without Faye, these books would not have been possible.

I had the best team of editors around: Diane Foster, Stacy Wagner, and Kris Bergstad. You took my words and you gave them power. Thank you.

Thanks to my wonderful Board Chairman at Strategic Teaching and Learning, Dulany Howland: Thank you for sticking with me in the good times and the tough spots. Your expertise and friendship have been invaluable.

To my dear friend, Mark Buchanan,
who has great insights into human behavior

Introduction

Off-task behavior in the classroom costs so much in terms of time on task, not to mention the emotional cost on teachers and other students in the classroom. About 98% of the behavior problems in the classroom are identified as simple off-task behavior. While the problem can be considered minor in terms of today's kids, the amount of lost learning time is not minor. Off-task behavior includes everything from pencil tapping, sleeping, talking to neighbors, and passing notes, to not paying attention. Most of these behavior problems can be prevented thorough a series of brain-compatible procedures carried out by the classroom teacher. We know, through brain research, why the brain pays attention and at least some of the reasons why we lose student attention.

The purpose of this book is to look at the various types of behavior problems in the classroom, possible root causes, and ways to deal with the problems effectively. The material is not intended to provide a quick fix, but rather to guide the classroom teacher as he or she works to help students become aware of their own behaviors and to be responsible for them. Good classroom managers are easy to spot because they have characteristics that lead students to become good self-managers. In the chapters to follow, we will look at seven ways to prevent simple off-task behavior, as well as what to do when the behavior is more than just off task.

We will also view behavior in terms of brain research. Of the three systems of the brain, the self-system has the greatest effect on student success. This is also the system of the brain that controls whether we pay attention, whether we involve ourselves in the learning, and whether we tap into intrinsic motivation. A wise teacher uses this system of the brain to turn her students on to learning.

Sometimes, behavior problems go beyond the simple off-task variety and must be addressed immediately. When that occurs, it is important that the teacher respond appropriately in voice and in body language to get the student back on task as quickly as possible. Some specific techniques will be provided in the pages to come.

Working with urban learners can be challenging to the teacher who does not know or understand that the cognitive structures will not be in place until students specifically understand the hidden rules and until they feel accepted in the classroom. Students must know that the set of rules for the classroom and the workplace is different from the rules for the street. They need to know how to survive in each.

The teacher who has a plan for behavior will be better able to control impulsivity in students and is more likely to maximize the learning time and the quality of learning.

Meta-analysis studies have proven that teaching vocabulary first helps students to learn and has a strong impact on making students successful. With that in mind, I am providing a list of the vocabulary related to this book. In Form 0.1, write what you already know about the vocabulary words. After you have read the book and reviewed the glossary, come back to your original list and see if you want to change or add to your earlier definitions. I am also providing a pre-test for you to help you determine your level of expertise in advance.

Form 0.1   Vocabulary list for Classroom Management and Discipline

Vocabulary	Your Definition	Your Revised Definition
Assessment of behavior		
At-risk		
Body language		
Classroom management		
Cooperative learning		
Corporal punishment		
Efficacy		
Emotion		
Emotional intelligence		
Hidden rules		
Impulsivity		
Modalities		
Poverty		
Rewards and punishments		
Self-management		
Study groups		
Temporary groups		
Thinking systems		
Voices		

Vocabulary
Pre-Test

Instructions: Choose the one *best* answer for the questions provided.

1. Self-management skills are regulated by the . . .
   A. Self-system
   B. Metacognitive system
   C. Cognitive system
   D. Regulatory system

2. Efficacy relates to . . .
   A. Past success
   B. The regulatory system
   C. Empathy
   D. Heredity

3. Most students are . . .
   A. Kinesthetic
   B. Auditory
   C. Visual
   D. Olfactory

4. The best structure for the classroom is . . .
   A. Independent learning
   B. Cooperative learning
   C. Competitive learning
   D. A combination of all three structures

5. Which characteristic is not true of temporary groups?
   A. Meet every day
   B. Meet for a short segment of time
   C. Support one another
   D. Incorporate social skills

6. Which of the following characteristics is not an indicator of being at risk?
   A. Economic conditions
   B. Past failure
   C. Reading skills
   D. Single-parent home

7. Hidden rules relate to . . .
   A. Class norms that are not posted
   B. Schools that do not use rubrics
   C. Socioeconomic groups
   D. Parents who are uninformed

8. Having empathy for others is a characteristic of . . .
   A. Emotional intelligence
   B. The cognitive system
   C. Modalities
   D. Impulsivity

9. Intrinsic motivation is . . .
   A. Based on rewards
   B. Controlled in the self-system
   C. Controlled in the cognitive system
   D. Controlled in the metacognitive system

10. Which of the following is true of learning states?
    A. Students need low challenge.
    B. Students need low stress.
    C. Students need no stress.
    D. Students do not need challenge.

11. Which of the following statements is *true* of cooperative learning?
    A. We practice cooperative learning when we put students into groups.
    B. Cooperative learning always includes social skills.

C. Cooperative learning groups are usually groups of four.

D. Cooperative learning should be a part of every lesson.

12. Students who quit a project because they have a problem that they cannot solve are demonstrating . . .
    A. Metacognitive problems
    B. Impulsivity
    C. The child voice
    D. Cognitive problems

13. A teacher who has been lecturing in the classroom for 20 minutes decides to put the students into study groups to learn the additional information. This teacher is most probably . . .
    A. At the end of the class time
    B. Introducing the unit
    C. Practicing goal setting
    D. Changing learning states

14. If a teacher has asked the students to practice the learning by building models, which system of the brain is going to be most important in monitoring the learning?
    A. Self
    B. Metacognitive
    C. Cognitive
    D. Experimental

15. When we are angry we should keep our hands . . .
    A. Behind our back
    B. Above our waist
    C. At our sides
    D. Folded

16. Mr. Walters has been cruising his classroom to help students when he notices that a student has turned around in his desk to talk to another student. Mr. Walters walks to the student's desk. What should he do next?

A. Stare at the student.
B. Ask the student to step into the hall.
C. Speak to the student so that everyone can hear.
D. Put his palms on the student's desk.

17. When Mr. Walters starts to move away from the student's desk, he notices that the student has turned only partially around toward her desk. What does this usually indicate?
    A. The student will go back to talking to her neighbor when Mr. Walters walks away.
    B. The student is not comfortable in the room.
    C. The student feels dejected.
    D. The student is insecure with the situation.

18. Once the student goes back to work, Mr. Walters thanks her for working and then turns to walk away. He hears the student say, "Yeah, like I care." Mr. Walters should . . .
    A. Ignore the student and keep walking.
    B. Send the student to the office.
    C. Go back to the student and get her back on task.
    D. Respond to the comment.

19. When asking oral questions, which is it important that a teacher *not* do?
    A. Provide less wait time for brighter students.
    B. Restate the question when students do not know the answer.
    C. Give credit for partial answers.
    D. Refrain from calling on at-risk students.

20. Which of the following is *not* true of intelligence? Intelligence is . . .
    A. The ability to solve problems that one encounters in real life
    B. The ability to generate new problems to solve
    C. The ability to make something or offer a service that is valued within one's culture
    D. Fixed at birth

1

Old-Fashioned Discipline

"The old theory, we can make 'em work; all we have to do is get tough, has never produced intellectual effort in the history of the world, and it certainly won't work in this situation."

—Glasser, cited in Gough,
The Key to Improving Schools, 1987

Behavior models of the past were based on a system of rewards and punishments intended to change negative actions to positive. Students were rewarded for good behavior and were punished for poor behavior. Reaction to discipline problems were often more knee-jerk than planned and were not necessarily based on what was best for the student. The prevailing attitude was too often, "My way or the highway." Students responded in kind, by often choosing the highway. Students who were punished frequently tended to leave school early for jobs that did not require a high school diploma, or they became a part of the problems of the street. Today, federal and state laws prevent students from dropping out of school early. We know that the model of the past that was based on "my way or the highway" does not work with today's students, and that sending students to the streets leads to a significant waste of lives and resources. Glasser (1986) says, "Prior to WWII, we didn't have specific discipline programs. We maintained order in schools by throwing out the unruly and flunking out the unmotivated. Now we keep those students in school and try to find ways to keep them quiet."

Models of the past that were based on stimulus/response or reward and punishment techniques worked for students who were motivated to learn, but they were a dismal failure for those students whose needs were not being met or who learn differently. Curwin and Mendler (1988) define the models of the past as the "obedience models" because they were built on teachers' gaining power over students through intimidation and punishment in order to coerce obedience. Curwin and Mendler say, "In the short term, obedience offers teachers relief, a sense of power and control, and an oasis from the constant bombardment of defiance. In the long run, however, obedience leads to student immaturity, a lack of responsibility, an inability to think clearly and critically, and a feeling of helplessness that is manifested by withdrawal, aggressiveness, or power struggles." Burke (1992) adds, "Not getting caught supercedes everything else in the game of teacher versus student."

Teachers today know that the obedience model not only does not work for about half of the students, it is also not brain compatible for changing negative behavior and in building emotional intelligence. The Master Teacher (2002) says that any classroom management program today should include three teacher actions.

First, any discipline program should include provisions for teaching students self-discipline processes. Master Teacher explains, "We can't assume that our students will learn appropriate behavior simply by pointing out inappropriate behavior. Neither can we assume that criticizing, reprimanding, and punishing students for inappropriate behavior will make them change."

Second, students must know, in advance, our expectations in terms of both academics and behaviors. Unfortunately, what is acceptable in one classroom is not necessarily acceptable in another, so we must specifically teach students the expectations. To the extent possible, these rules should be kept brief, written in the positive, and displayed in the classroom.

Third, the expected behaviors should fit the situation. For example, behavior that is acceptable when students are reading silently is not the same as behavior expected when students are working in small groups. By the same token, behavior in the classroom is not the same as behavior in the lunchroom or in the gym. The more that teachers and administrators can come to consensus on behavior expectations for the school, the smoother the transition from one situation to the other will be. In the classroom make sure that students understand the expectations for different learning situations. For example, a class rule such as "no talking" does not make sense in light of a brain compatible classroom where students are encouraged to interact at various points in the learning.

In the chapters to follow, we will look at a model for building emotional- and self-awareness in students so that students are responsible for their behavior and for their learning as well. We will examine the characteristics of good classroom management and how to build self-management in students. A process for helping to prevent off-task behavior while keeping yourself under control, as well as guidelines for solving more difficult discipline problems will be included. In Chapter 6, a step-by-step guide for setting good discipline management standards is provided to get you started on a plan for your classroom.

2

The Basis for Off-Task Behavior

"More than any other system, the emotional learning system of the brain outwardly defines the individual and sets the stage for how people interact with others, learn, behave, and reflect on their circumstances."

—Barbara Given, *Teaching to the Brain's Natural Learning Systems*, p. 15.

Jensen (1997) says that most so-called behavior problems in the classroom are not really behavior problems, but simply off-task behavior as a result of problems with the learning. When we do not see the relevance in the learning, are bored, or have high anxiety over the material, we tend to drop out mentally. It is in these states that off-task behavior occurs. Think of a time you were in a classroom, meeting, or training in which the information was either boring, not well presented, or not relevant to you personally. What did you do? Did you talk to your neighbor, sleep, or perform other tasks? We should not be surprised that our students exhibit some of these same behaviors in the face of the same kinds of situations.

On Task From the Beginning

Once class begins and we stand to provide information or directions for the lesson, the brain makes crucial decisions about whether or not attention will be focused on the learning. We are in competition with all of the other factors on which our students want to focus attention, including upcoming activities, other students in the room, and incoming stimulus from the senses. The brain cannot and will not attend to all of these factors at once; it will make choices. We want the learning to be its first choice.

Jensen (1997) says that for students to attend to learning they must (a) be intrinsically motivated, (b) be in an immersed flow state, and (c) have low stress. Let's look at each of these factors in light of helping students to be successful from the beginning.

Intrinsic Motivation

Since 98% of the learning comes to us through the senses, as teachers we want to use a variety of sensory stimuli to gain our students' attention to the learning. Whether we gain attention through visual, auditory, olfactory, touch, taste, or a combination, within a matter of seconds, our students' brains will decide whether or not they will pay attention to the learning. This motivation to learn is controlled by the self-system of the brain. When Marzano (1998) released his research on meta-analyses of the teaching practices that have the most effect on student learning, he and his colleagues found that the greatest amount of student success comes from the self-system. There is empirical evidence to prove that not only should learning begin in the self-system of the brain, the self-system should be directly attended to prior to the learning:

Specifically, in a recent meta-analysis involving over 2,500 effect sizes, instructional strategies were analyzed as to which of the systems of the brain have the greatest impact on learning. For example, if an instructional strategy addressed student beliefs and attitudes, it was coded as employing the self-system. If an instructional technique addressed the establishment of goals, it was coded as employing the metacognitive system. Finally, if the instructional technique addressed the analysis of information, it was coded as employing the cognitive system. (Marzano, Pickering, & Pollock, 2001)

Of these three systems, it was found that the self-system had the greatest effect on student success. In fact, the self-system, when used appropriately, can raise the learning level of a student from the 50th percentile to the 77th percentile. The metacognitive system was second (76th percentile), and the cognitive system was last in terms of effect size (71st percentile).

THE SELF-SYSTEM AND BEHAVIOR

The self-system is composed of attitudes, emotions, and beliefs that are at the heart of intrinsic motivation. This system determines whether students will pay attention, whether they will engage in the tasks, and whether they will bring energy to the assignment. Four components make up the self-system, and each is important in the decisions of the learner about on-task behavior.

The first component of the self-system is importance. In order for the learner to pay attention, learners must believe that the knowledge or task is relevant to them and that it is important to know and/or be able to do. The task should also be appropriately challenging. Tomlinson (1999) says, "A task is appropriately challenging when it asks learners to risk a leap into the unknown, but they know enough to get started and have additional support for reaching a new level of understanding." Students must believe that they have enough information and the resources to be successful if they work hard. Tomlinson (1999) continues, "Students who consistently fail lose their motivation to learn. Students who succeed too easily also lose their motivation to learn."

The second component is efficacy. Efficacy is the belief, by the learner, that he or she can do the task or learn the information. The belief is based, in part, on past experience. This is one of the reasons it is important that students experience success. Because it builds self-efficacy in students, success really does breed success. Self-efficacy differs from self-esteem in that self-esteem is a belief in oneself, while self-efficacy is a belief that we can do something because we have been successful before. Self-efficacy is more powerful because it is based on specific evidence from past experience. We build self-efficacy in students by giving them specific feedback so that they can be successful. Students need to know what they did right and upon what they can improve. This is extremely important if we are to move students to high achievement.

We often see a sense of helplessness in students from poverty. The prevailing attitude, learned at an early age, is that the family has no control over their plight in life, which they cannot improve, and that poverty is their destiny. As Sprenger (2002) says, "Learned helplessness is a disorder in which cause and effect no longer connect to the child's brain." Remember that helplessness is a learned condition; it is not genetic. We can help students to rewire from learned helplessness to a sense of positive self-efficacy. Jensen (1997) suggests that the teacher begin with an easy task and continue to upgrade until the task is challenging and the stress level is moderate or low. How can we have tasks that are difficult and stress levels that are moderate or low? By providing the scaffolding necessary to tackle difficult tasks. The scaffolding is provided as we gradually elevate the difficulty of the task rather than beginning with high difficulty.

When students do not believe that they can learn, there are specific tactics that can be employed to help convince learners of what they know. Jensen (1997) says, "The self-convincer function is especially critical when it comes to changing a learner's beliefs. If a student already believes that he or she is going to succeed, it takes only 'maintenance reinforcement' to preserve that belief." He goes on to say that for slow learners or for the student who believes that he or she is a failure, there are three knowledge criteria that must be met to convince him or her otherwise. The three knowledge criteria to which Jensen refers are:

- Reinforcement of new information in the learners' preferred modality. Information enters the brain through the senses. Most of us have a modality in which we prefer to receive information. When we are taught in that modality, we are more comfortable, and we have a better flow state. For visual learners (the largest number of students in the classroom), being able to see how the math works, or visually seeing the learning in some way, helps them to be convinced that they know it. If you are re-teaching students who did not "get it" the first time, you will probably not reach them until you teach in their preferred (most comfortable) modality. One reason so many students do not do well in the classroom is that they are taught and re-taught in the same way. Provide more than one teaching method for teaching new material so that you teach to all students. Organizers are a great way to reinforce the learning with your students. Most organizers are either linguistic (using words to convey the information) or nonlinguistic (relying on structure rather than words to convey the information). An example of a linguistic organizer is a learning log in which students record their thoughts, interpretations, ideas, and questions about the learning. A nonlinguistic organizer might be a mind map or a flowchart. The effect size of organizers is impressive. The McREL study as reported by Marzano (1998) shows that using organizers in general will raise the student achievement for the given learning from the 50th percentile to the 72nd percentile and using nonlinguistic representations of the learning will raise that same student to the 77th percentile. It is significant when we can take a student from nonachievement (50th percentile) to an acceptable achievement level in most states (77th percentile) by adding visual organizers. These data should not be surprising since we know from the studies reported by Jensen (1997) that at least 87% of the students in most classrooms are visual learners.

- The second criterion to convince the brain that it knows the learning is through adequate practice. The first practices should be under the direction of the teacher with constructive, specific feedback. Some students need to practice only a few times to internalize the information, while others may need to practice more times before the learning is meaningful to them. If students are having difficulty grasping the concept or task, try changing the mode in which you are teaching. For example, if you have been using words to teach, try using pictures or models. One of the difficulties that we encounter in working with students from poverty and with English language learners is that they do not have the language acquisition skills to learn in a classroom dominated by auditory teaching and learning. Payne (2001) says that students who know only the casual talk of the streets do not use or have many prepositions or adverbs in their speech. She goes on to say, "If a student does not have specific words to use, then his/her ability to retrieve and use information is severely limited. It is not enough that a student can do a task, he/she must also be able to label the procedures, tasks, and processes so that the task can be successfully repeated each time and analyzed at a metacognitive level." For these students we must model the use of appropriate labels and guide them to identify the correct words for specific processes. We need to rely on visual and kinesthetic methods of teaching until these students have the verbal skills to grasp the learning.

- The third convincer is to provide enough time for the brain to give meaning to the learning. Provide adequate time for students to process the new information before moving them to independent practice.

Jensen (1997) says, "Once what we have learned in our preferred modality has been reinforced—the right number of times and for the right length of time—we will feel that it is true. Until then, it's purely data that lacks intrinsic meaning."

We want students to leave our classrooms knowing what they know. Jensen concludes, "These activities should incorporate all three learning modalities, last for several minutes or more, and be repeated several times. These criteria are often met through activities like peer teaching, role playing, journal writing, self-assessment exercises and group work."

The third component of the self-system is emotional response. Many researchers believe that emotion is the strongest force in the brain. Emotion can literally shut down the higher-level functions of the brain when the learner is under great stress. It can also enhance the learning so that it is remembered with higher clarity. Dozier (1998) says, "The partnership between the emotional and cognitive systems rapidly produces an emotional first impression of everything we experience; that input is monitored with regard to whether we like or dislike it. When the dislike is intense, the primitive fear reaction of flight or fight is triggered." Thus it is important that students feel good about the learning and about the classroom. Given (2002) says, "A steady diet of fear, either triggered through actual events or generated vicariously, dramatically diminishes a person's ability to use other learning systems effectively." Students who are labeled as "troublemakers" may, in fact, be operating out of fear. Given (2002) explains,

> The outward manifestations of personal fear can be masked as misbehavior, nonresponsiveness, lack of motivation, and other chronic behavior patterns. These traits may look like a negative attitude rather than a coping strategy against the fear of failure, the fear of social isolation, the fear of an angry parent, or any number of other fears that children fail to understand and cannot effectively articulate.

The fourth component of the self-system is overall motivation. Overall motivation occurs when learners believe the learning is important, when learners believe that they can accomplish the task, and when there is a strong positive emotion toward the learning.

Remember, all learning begins in the self-system when the learner decides to pay attention, to undertake the task of learning, and to initiate the first steps of the task.

FLOW STATE

The second criterion for learning, presented by Jensen (1997), is appropriate flow state. Psychologist Mihaly Csikszentmihalyi (1990) says that optimal learning occurs in a "flow state," which he defines as "a pattern of activity in which individual or group goals emerge naturally as a result of a pleasurable activity and interaction with the environment." Jensen (1997) describes "This uninterrupted state in which one 'loses oneself' in the performance is well known as a timeless, pleasure-producing experience. Children, teenagers and athletes often reach this flow state more easily than the average adult; and therefore, maximize creativity and learning." Think of a time when you were learning something new. How did you feel about the learning? Were you so wrapped up in the task or learning that time passed quickly and you did not want to be interrupted? Jensen says, "When learner's skills, attention, environment, and will are all matched up with the task at hand, they are in the 'flow.'"

Several years ago, I was involved in a restructuring project in a school that had low test scores, a high dropout rate, and poor attendance. We literally turned the school upside down and shook it in terms of changing the climate, the way we assessed, and the way we taught our students. Within three months, scores were coming up and the attendance rate jumped to almost 98 percent. Over time the scores zoomed to the top in our state, to the point that we constantly had visitors in the school to see what we were doing. One morning, the state commissioner of education and members of the state board of education visited the school. I was with the commissioner when he entered one of the classrooms. High school students were working in small groups on projects in English. They totally ignored the commissioner because they were so involved in talking to each other and in planning. Finally, the commissioner pulled a chair into one of the groups and introduced himself to get their attention and to find out what they were doing. Everyone wants this kind of classroom, and the reality is that it is possible. If we could make it happen in a school where 50% of the students qualified for free or reduced lunch and where test scores and climate had been so poor they had been cited by the state, it can be done throughout this country.

You may be thinking at this point that you wish your students would exhibit this behavior in the classroom, but the reality may be that they do not. Let's look at some strategies that have been proven to help move students into this flow state and why they seem to work.

Flow state seems to be regulated, in part, by the metacognitive system of the brain. It is in this system that students set personal goals for the learning and monitor their activities. It is also this system that makes the decision whether or not to remain on task even when the learner is tired or frustrated. This system also regulates our ability to control impulsivity. Once the self-system has decided to pay attention to the learning, the metacognitive system takes over. Let's look at the components of this system and how we can move students to stay on task.

The first component of this system is goal specification. Once students have been given a task, it is this component that builds a goal for the task. For example, if the teacher has assigned a math problem for students to work, they will set a goal for how to work the problem based on the algorithms, tactics, or heuristics that have been taught. If they have not been taught the necessary information sufficiently, frustration will set in and off-task behavior will emerge. While this function is done unconsciously within the brain, we can better ensure success by explicitly teaching students to set goals and to think through what they will need to know and do in order to carry out those goals. Setting goals builds motivation to complete the task. Many times students will begin a task only to throw up their hands and quit once they encounter problems. We refer to this as impulsivity. According to Payne (2001), impulsivity is a characteristic often found in students raised in poverty. These children have observed the attitudes of the adults around them, which are often built on failed hopes and a feeling of loss of control. Add to that the stress associated with trying to survive in violent, aggressive, or depressed conditions, and we have a formula for trouble.

The second component of the metacognitive system is process monitoring. This component deals only with procedural knowledge. Procedural knowledge is the process of doing something with the information. For example, when we are teaching students facts, dates, vocabulary, and so on, we are teaching them declarative knowledge, or the "what" of learning. When we ask students to perform experiments, work problems, write themes, and so on, we are teaching procedural knowledge, or the "how" of learning. Process monitoring checks to see that the algorithms, tactics, or processes being used to carry out the tasks are working effectively. For example, a student working on a math assignment employs the algorithms taught that day in the classroom for working the problems. When the student has difficulty with one of the problems, the process employed comes into question. If the student encounters a snag in the process with this particular problem, process monitoring in the brain will raise a red flag that something is wrong. If students have not learned to control impulsivity, they may throw up their hands and give up rather than figure out what must be done to solve the problem. Payne (2001) says, "There is a direct correlation between impulse control and improved behavior and achievement." This means that by specifically teaching goal setting and by providing a model for students to make choices when things do not go well, we can improve both cognitive and behavioral skills in our students. One way you can do this is to incorporate goal setting into each lesson. For example, at the elementary level if I were teaching a lesson on shapes, I would first show my students my goals for the lesson. Those goals should be based on state and national standards that should be displayed in the classroom (send them home to parents as well). The goals might look something like this:

Standard 5.2: Students will identify a circle, square, cylinder, triangle, rectangle, and cone.

Goals for Learning:

Students will know (declarative knowledge):

1. The characteristics of a circle, square, cylinder, triangle, rectangle, and cone.

2. Ways that a circle, square, cylinder, triangle, rectangle, and cone are alike and different.

3. How circles, cylinders, triangles, rectangles, and cones are used in everyday life.

Students will be able to (procedural knowledge):

1. Identify a circle, square, cylinder, triangle, rectangle, and cone.

2. Draw each of the shapes accurately.

3. Identify each of the shapes in a given environment (e.g., outside, in the classroom, etc.).

Ask students to set personal goals for the learning, and provide specific feedback to students on how they are doing in regard to reaching their goals.

Directly teach students techniques for monitoring their own work and for making changes to a plan as needed.

Form 2.1 shows a simple outline to help students learn to plan. Planning prevents students from "blowing up" when they cannot do the work and from giving up when the work becomes difficult. It has been said that one of the ways society judges whether we are "smart" is our ability to make changes in a plan when it is not working and to complete tasks with high energy.

The third and fourth components of the metacognition system are monitoring clarity and accuracy. These components are also associated with intelligent behavior. It is through these two components that the learner carries out the task by adjusting the original goal when needed. Being able to complete a task at a quality level requires that students know how to monitor and adjust as needed. This is a skill that must be explicitly taught whether your students are six or sixteen. Tasks should be challenging, but not frustrating. We accomplish this by giving our students the resources necessary to complete the task and by adding difficulty in incremental steps. Jensen (1997) uses the example of learning to play a new instrument. If the learner tried to play a piece of music from the beginning, the challenge would be high but the stress level would also be so high that the learner might quit. Learning to plan an instrument begins with learning the instrument itself and then with scales, and so on. Each time the challenge is maintained, but the stress is moderate or low because the tasks are in sequence. Csikszentmihalyi (1990) says, "When challenges are greater than your skills, that's anxiety. When your skills exceed the challenges, that's boredom." We also help prevent impulsivity by giving specific and frequent feedback. Marzano (1998) found that when feedback is specific and constructive, it has a high effect on student learning. Marzano's meta-analysis shows that when specific feedback is given to students appropriately, it has the power to raise student achievement from the 50th percentile to the 77th percentile. Just saying "Great job" is not enough. As a matter of fact, that kind of general feedback has little or no effect on student learning and may have a negative effect when students know that they have not done their best work.

Form 2.1   Planning Tool

Your name ....

What is your goal? ....

....

....

What resources will you need to accomplish your goal?

....

....

....

Steps: What will you do?

First: ....

Second: ....

Third: ....

Fourth: ....

Fifth: ....

Sixth: ....

(Continued)

Form 2.1 Continued

Evaluation:

What went well with this plan? Did you accomplish your goal?

What went wrong?

What did you do when you encountered problems?

What will you do different next time?

Figure 2.1   The Systems of Thinking and Motivation

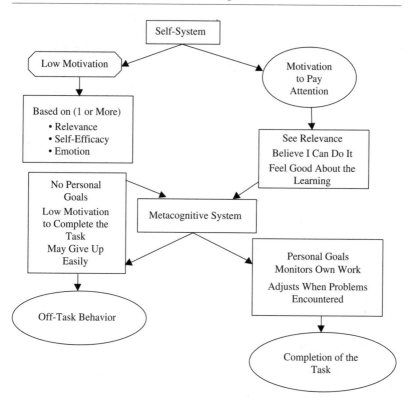

Figure 2.1 shows the importance of the self- and metacognitive systems to student behavior.

LOW TO MODERATE STRESS

The third criterion for student success is providing a climate in the classroom that is conducive to low or moderate stress—never high. From the time we were born, the brain has placed survival above all else. Jensen (1997) says that the brain stem is the director of our emotions under threat. "When threat is perceived, excessive cortisol is released into the body causing higher-order thinking skills to take a backseat to automatic functions that may help you survive." While the release of cortisol into the system during a time of great stress is helpful to us as a species, students who live in a situation of great stress all the time tend to be sick a great deal, and they tend to have less control of their impulses. Computer-generated images of individuals under great stress reveal that there is increased blood flow and electrical activity in the brain stem and cerebellum. Jensen (1997) says, "These physiological changes cause more predictable, rote, knee-jerk reactions when the brain senses any threat that induces helplessness." In order to find ways to prevent or reduce threat in the classroom, it is necessary to look at those factors that constitute threat. Stress or threat can be categorized as:

- Physical threat that can come from inside or outside the classroom.
- Emotional threat such as the fear of being embarrassed. For adolescents, one of the greatest fears is to be made to look foolish in front of their friends.
- Education threats such as fear of failure or not understanding the material well enough to carry out tasks.
- Resources that are so limited that they restrict the student's ability to be successful. Resource restriction may be anything from lack of language or verbal skills to unrealistic time deadlines for work.

In this day and time, providing low stress may seem impossible. We cannot control our students' lives outside the classroom, but we do have tremendous control over the quality of their lives for seven or more hours each day. What are some things that you can do in your classroom to lower the stress level of your students?

An Ounce of Prevention

All discipline situations have three variables: the teacher, the problem student, and the rest of the class. Of these three variables, the one over which teachers have 100% control is themselves. The Master Teacher (2002) says, "Too often, our thinking is totally in terms of student adjustment. Seldom do we think predominately in terms of teacher adjustment."

As teachers we are in tune with our students' body language, and we know when it is time to change what we are doing before boredom or disinterest takes over. A wise teacher will make changes so that behavior problems do not occur. At the outset, I have said that most of the off-task behavior in the classroom is not related to the desire to be undisciplined but occurs as a result of other factors. Master Teacher (2002) continues, "To be an effective disciplinarian, the teacher must become the primary adjuster. A teacher can be successful in getting students to adjust their behavior only by first adjusting his or her own behavior." Jensen (1997) provides seven tools to use in order to prevent off-task behavior. I have used these in my classroom and in my workshops with teachers. Next time your students begin to fade on you, do one or more of the following: Change the timing of the activities, change the activities, change the environment, add a variety of resources, change who is in charge of the teaching, change the tone or the focus.

EXAMINE TIMING

Our brain is not wired to listen attentively for long stretches of time. Jensen (1997) explains that our brain is good at immediate change and trends but not very good at discerning slow trends. "This provides us with a biological explanation of why expecting extended classroom attention is problematic and even inappropriate." In the literature you will see various formulas for limits for the amount of time spent on direct instruction before moving to a different activity. I have found the following rule to work best with all ages of students: Use the students' ages. For example, if the students are eight, talk for only eight minutes before changing to a different activity. If the students are 15 through adult, 20 minutes is about as long as they can listen actively before becoming fidgety or talking to their neighbor. All of this information is backed up by brain research. I call it the brain's body clock because it seems to fade out if we go over the time limit. Watch your students as you talk to them. Do they become fidgety, do they begin to talk to one another, or do they look down as if looking for something else to do? I have just described off-task behavior for the kinesthetic learner, the verbal learner, and the visual learner, respectively.

EXAMINE THE ACTIVITY

If you have been talking, change directions so that students are working in small group discussions, or provide activities that involve processes you are discussing. If you have a great deal of information that you must provide and you are unsure about other methods, here is a simple technique to use.

- Place students in pairs and designate one of the partners as partner A and the other as partner B.
- Tell the partner A students to tell partner B everything they can remember that was discussed in the last 20 minutes.
- Next, ask partner B students to tell partner A everything they can remember that was discussed in the last 20 minutes that partner A left out.

A variation of this technique that I often use with my college and adult classes is to break them into learning groups of three, four, or five. (With young learners, do not use groups larger than three—you will thank me.) Next assign each group a different task, such as:

- Group 1—As I talk, take notes that you will compress to summarize the information for the class.
- Group 2—As I talk, make notes so that you can come up with a list of questions for further discussion.

- Group 3—As I talk, make notes so that you can come up with some vocabulary that will be important to know as we study this lesson.
- Group 4—What are the possible problem areas for this lesson? What will need further clarification or discussion?
- Group 5—You will critique the work of the other groups. What did they leave out? How well did they follow the directions? Do you think they were active or passive listeners?

Of course, there are many variations to this technique. The point is that by giving the students a goal, you have helped them to use their natural internal motivation to learn.

Sometimes just asking the students to stand and stretch will change the rhythm of the learning and increase attention. If the students are sleepy, have them stand to talk to their partner. This raises the oxygen level to the brain and helps students to be more alert. The old adage "We think better on our feet" is absolutely true.

As a final note on changing activities, remember that kinesthetic students need movement. If they are required to sit passively in a classroom while the teacher imparts words for long stretches of time, they may become discipline problems. The traditional teacher (one who relies on lecture, note taking, and homework for teaching tools) will be frustrated by the kinesthetic learners in the classroom. Another mistake often made in the classroom is to assume that learners who are not looking at us as we speak are not paying attention. Visual learners often do not look at the speaker, but that does not mean they are not listening.

EXAMINE THE ENVIRONMENT

Stand at the door of your classroom and look at the room. What is the first thing that students see as they enter your room? What is the lighting—dim, bright, fluorescent? How does the room smell? What are the sounds of the room? How is seating arranged?

The classroom should be an inviting place, well lit, clean, and orderly. You can change the smell of the room with ionizers (fresh, clean smell—like after a lightning storm) or with gel candles (unlit).

The lighting of the room has been a subject for discussion for years. Current thought is that a combination of natural light and indoor light (not fluorescent) is best for learning.

The brain likes novelty, so change the arrangement of the room from time to time. One of our memory pathways (episodic) attaches learning to context. Changing the seating arrangement after each unit or series of lessons will help activate this pathway to strengthen the learning. This pathway has another effect on behavior. Next time you have a student who is off task several times, try moving the student to the other side of the room before asking for a stop to pencil tapping, kicking the desk, or whatever constituted the off-task behavior. Just moving students to the other side of the room gives them a fresh start, as if they were in a different classroom. Don't believe me? Do you always sit in the same place for faculty meeting, church service, or club meeting? Next time you go, move to the opposite side of the room. If you are like most of us, you will experience the phenomenon of being in a completely different place.

Examine the Resources

Just changing the mode of presentation can make a huge difference in attention. Bring in books, tapes, projection devices, computers, and music. Music has a tremendous emotional impact on our brain. It can help to strengthen the learning and provide positive emotions. Try incorporating "sounds of the times" into a lesson on history or on periods in literature.

Use People

Use other resources besides yourself for teaching. Bring in guest speakers or ask your students to teach parts of the lesson. When did you best know the subject you teach? Probably when you taught it. By providing opportunities for students to teach the whole class, to partners, or to groups, we help them to strengthen the learning.

Use Tone

Change the tone of the lesson by using themes for the learning. The teacher of the year in my area teaches reading and writing in an inner-city middle school. Every year she teaches around a theme. Her classroom reflects the theme and the lessons are built around the theme. This year her theme, was "Games." She built student activities around games such as Scrabble (for vocabulary), and she rides a scooter in the classroom as she goes from student to student to provide feedback on their work. It does not take away from learning; just the opposite—her inner-city kids are knocking the top off of their assessments. She says that there are days when she dismisses her classes and they don't want to leave.

Another way to change tone is by timing activities so that students have the time to complete their activities, but not enough time to talk about what they will do after school. Bring in resources other than just the text. Set goals and have your students set goals for learning—and check often to see that you are all meeting your goals.

Change the Focus

Use exercises at the beginning of class or throughout the day to keep students on-task.

Visualization and mental pictures are important to learning. Teach students how to visualize the learning and/or tasks before they begin. Basketball players who have never visualized themselves shooting a basket will have a more difficult time than players who have a mental picture of making the shot.

Last, explicitly teach students about learning states so that they can monitor their own learning and behavior. Jensen (1997) recommends having students "consciously experience the everyday states of anticipation, curiosity, confusion, happiness, suspicion, concentration, frustration, anger or apathy. Then help them recognize that they, not you, control their states."

3

Dealing With Difficult Students

Whille the ideas provided in the previous chapters work most of the time, there are always those times when we need to move to Plan B. Not all off-task problems in the classroom are minor. While there are many reasons for student behavior, most writers place the types of negative behavior into basic categories for discussion. Let's look at some of the categories of negative behavior and the characteristics that usually accompany those behaviors.

STUDENTS WHO WANT ATTENTION

Students who are not getting the attention that they want (or need) through normal means may resort to off-task, attention-getting behavior to accomplish their goal. Some of the ways in which they exhibit this behavior include:

- Being late for class
- Speaking out without permission

- Making noises
- Talking out of turn
- Getting up from their desks or chairs to walk around or to go to the pencil sharpener, trashcan, and so forth, for the third or fourth time
- Intentionally breaking the rules

When needs are not met, the behavior may escalate to:

- Shouts and verbal attacks
- Defiance of authority

You will know this behavior by the effect that it has on you, the teacher: "When attention is the reason for the misbehavior, you will generally feel annoyed" (Master Teacher, 2002).

While there is no single solution to the attention-getting behavior of some of our students, examining some of the reasons for this behavior may help in finding solutions. These students are often kinesthetic learners or highly visual learners who have difficulty in a classroom where the dominant teaching method is auditory. By bringing in visuals, models of the learning, and providing movement, the classroom teacher may be able to solve this dilemma. Boredom often causes off-task, attention-getting behavior. Ask yourself, is this student being challenged? Have students been required to sit and listen for long periods of time? Brain researchers agree that our brain is not wired to attend to lecture-type formats for long periods of time. For students 15 years old through adult, 20 minutes seems to be the maximum time that we will pay attention in one segment. For students under 15, their age is a good measurement. For example, an eight-year-old will listen for about eight minutes before fading out. Have you been in a meeting in which someone talked to you for an hour or more? Did you notice yourself drifting in and out of the meeting even if the information was something of interest to you?

Help attention seekers to find fulfillment of their needs by providing feedback and lots of praise when they are working well. These students are like those people who pour quarters into video games—they do better when they have immediate feedback and instant gratification. These students also must be explicitly taught how to use the metacognitive system more appropriately, especially in regard to following through on tasks.

When working with students who want attention, it is important to remember the following points to turn the behavior around:

- Be direct and to the point. Tell them exactly what they did wrong, what the consequence is, and why.
- Lighten up. Smile or use humor when dealing with these students.
- Use negotiation when appropriate. For example, tell them that you will not lecture for more than ten minutes at a time and that you will provide opportunities for movement and for talking with other students through small groups or pairing of students at the end of each ten-minute segment. (This is a much more brain-friendly way to teach, anyway.)
- Provide opportunities for students to move during the class time. If working in groups is not appropriate to the learning, provide times when students can stand and stretch.

STUDENTS WHO SEEK POWER

Characteristics of students who seek power may include some or all of the following:

- Demonstrates anxiety
- May be tired often or have headaches
- May try to use guilt to get control
- Nags and complains often
- Tries to control the teacher or others in the classroom
- Has an authoritarian attitude

"When power is the reason for the misbehavior, you will generally feel threatened" (Master Teacher, 2002).

The play for power is usually made out of fear—fear of failure, fear of not being accepted, fear of consequences, and more. The teacher is usually the one with the most power in the classroom. After all, in the eyes of the students, this is the person who can give detentions, call parents, take away points, and give extra work. Interestingly, these are sometimes students who are very structured and who feel that the classroom does not provide enough structure or that discipline is not being maintained. These students will literally take over if intervention is not made promptly. Some ways that the classroom teacher can deal with this behavior is first to have very specific structures in place for work and behavior and to be consistent in their enforcement. Second, the teacher who provides choices for students and who involves students in classroom decisions is less likely to have this type of problem in the classroom. Getting into a power play with a student is a lose/lose situation. Even if you win, you will probably come across as a bully. A more powerful way to deal with these students is to listen to their concerns, acknowledge their feelings, and deal with the issue in private. If they complain loudly about you, let it go in one ear and out the other. Do not give in to the urge to get into a power struggle in front of the class. Help this student to see other choices in the situation. Payne (2001) says in working with inner-city students to have them write down other choices and which choice they will take next time. Glasser (1986) says students sometimes feel the need for power in the classroom because they feel that no one is listening to them. Students who are not doing well academically will especially feel that they are unimportant to the system. Burke (1992) uses a graphic model to help analyze conflicts with students who seek power. For older students, this tool could be used as the basis of a discussion to help them see their behavior and to help analyze those factors that will help to diffuse the situation (see Figure 3.1).

When working with students who seek power, the following guide may help to diffuse the behavior:

Figure 3.1   Phases of a Power Struggle

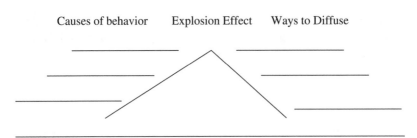

Causes of behavior   Explosion Effect   Ways to Diffuse

- Use direct honesty. Tell them exactly what the behavior looks like and sounds like. If you beat around the bush, they will know.
- Be factual. This is what you are doing and here are the indicators. These students do not want "I think and I feel"; they operate on facts.
- Refer back to the rules. These students usually like perimeters and rules and they like for them to be carried out. More than any other group, this group needs to see the rules and needs any disciplinary action to follow the rules.
- State the problem, the rules, and the consequences—in writing.

STUDENTS WHO WANT REVENGE

Some characteristics of students who seek revenge include:

- Critical of the classroom, other students, or the teacher
- Argumentative
- Questions why often
- Aloof or withdrawn, may even daydream
- Snobbish
- May do things his or her own way instead of the way that was assigned
- Critical of the rules, especially if they are inconsistent or if they are not enforced

When their behavior is out of control, it will manifest itself in acts of meanness or spitefulness such as beating up another student or defacing property. You will know the behavior by the way that it makes you feel. Most teachers will feel fearful or angry.

> Sometimes power seekers who never satisfy their need for power become revenge seekers to "get back" at the person or persons who thwarted their quest for power. Usually the revengeful student is trying to retaliate for something hurtful said by a parent, teacher, or peer or for some injustice or unfair deed. (Burke, 1992, p. 194)

The injustice may not have been done to the person seeking revenge—it may have been something that involved another student or the whole classroom. These students should be listened to and they should be taken seriously. Punitive actions toward this behavior will just accelerate the behavior in the student. The problem needs to be dealt with privately and in an adult voice—no put-downs, no sarcasm. These behaviors are sometimes manifested in some of our best students, especially if they feel that a wrong has been committed. These students can make the classroom a miserable place to be when they use their abilities to torpedo the climate in the classroom.

When working with students who seek revenge, the following suggestions may help to turn the behavior around:

- Use logic with these students. For example, "If I allow everyone in the room to 'do their own thing' instead of following the rules, we will have chaos."
- Be objective and nonconfrontational. Show respect for the student, not for the behavior.
- Acknowledge their contributions to the classroom.
- Provide opportunities for independent activities from time to time to help satisfy their need to do things their own way.

STUDENTS WHO FEEL INADEQUATE

Some of the characteristics of these students include:

- May ignore the teacher
- Does not participate
- May threaten to quit
- Tends to over-react to events
- May come to class unprepared or may not work to ability level
- Moody, blames others for failure

This behavior exhibited by your students may cause you to feel frustration.

These students are easy to spot in the classroom. Their emotions are usually on the outside. They may be more sensitive than other students and at times can be very caring of others. These students need frequent feedback about how they are doing, and they need positive encouragement. Often these are the underachievers who feel that they have no locus of control. They try hard but cannot experience success. Their frustration is manifested in tears, mentally dropping out, pouting, bursts of anger, or giving the teacher the silent treatment. The anxiety level needs to be lowered for these students by talking with them about why they feel inadequate, providing feedback and encouragement, and being sure that they have the necessary prerequisite skills before putting them into independent learning situations. Self-efficacy is the key to helping these students—provide incremental opportunities for these students to be successful, beginning with simple tasks with minimum challenge and working to high challenge but keeping low to moderate stress.

Some ideas for working with students who are motivated by feelings of inadequacy include:

- Talk to the student privately and in a calm tone.
- Listen to the student's side of the story.

- Keep communications open. These students usually like to talk and will shut down communication with you when they feel threatened.
- Help them to see the relevance of the learning, especially how it will help them personally and how it will help others.
- These students need feedback often, so to the extent possible, provide feedback throughout the class period.

For those problems that are motivated by anger, fear, revenge, or the need for power, we need a back-up plan. This plan should be built around planning for behavior problems and knowing in advance how you will handle them. When you have a plan, it is more likely that you will not explode or say something that will be difficult to follow up. Let me begin by telling you some things NOT to do.

- Do not lose your temper, even when students make comments about you or the classroom. Do not take it personally. Practice letting comments go in one ear and out the other. Before responding, count one hundred one, one hundred two, one hundred three. Take a breath and relax. Fred Jones (2002) says that we tend to move our hands above our waist when we are angry and we keep our hands at our side when we are relaxed. Practice being relaxed even when the situation is tense. Practice with your colleagues or family—anyone who is willing to help you learn to pace yourself and remain cool. If you take the comments personally, the situation is much more likely to escalate.
- Do not make idle threats. Never threaten action you cannot carry out. Even if you can carry out the threat, do not make it to the whole class—make it privately to the person(s) involved.
- Do not put names on the board. That just alienates the students.
- Do not humiliate the student.

- Do not ignore poor behavior. The class knows the behavior is inappropriate, and if you ignore it, the class will assume that behavior is not a priority with you.
- Never treat one student differently from another. Behavior management should be consistent and fair.

What if the discipline problems are persistent and/or not related to motivation? How should we deal with disruptive behavior?

Here are some guidelines for what to do to change disruptive behavior (based, in part, on the research of Fred Jones, available at www.fredjones.com).

1. Stay calm. Do not let your body language or your face betray the tension that you feel. Take time to calm down (even though it may seem like a long time, try giving yourself three seconds by counting one hundred one, one hundred two, one hundred three). Put your arms at your sides loosely and keep your jaw loose by running your tongue over the roof of your mouth.

2. Look toward the person or persons being disruptive. If that does not get them back to work, walk toward them.

3. When you have reached the student, put your palms down on the desk and speak quietly to the student. When the student gets back to work, remove your palms from the desk and slowly turn and leave. You should be cruising the room to help students and to see their work so that the students do not view this activity as an interruption. As a matter of fact, if done correctly, the students will not even be aware that you have disciplined a student.

4. Be sure that students who have been disruptive turn completely around to their work and have their feet under their desks. Students who turn only partially are probably planning to talk to their friends as soon as you walk away.

5. If a student makes a negative comment as you start to leave, calmly turn around and repeat the procedure you just did with that student. Do not answer the comment—why escalate the situation and allow them the victory of getting you angry? You must do something when the comment is made to get the student back on task, because not only have you heard the comment but so have students around you. They will be watching to see if you give in to the student.

6. Keep anecdotal notes in your grade book or in a separate notebook to help you keep up with encounters in case you must bring in parents or administration.

7. If you feel the behavior needs further discussion, ask the student to stay after class so that you may talk.

8. Keep your own file of students' names, addresses, phone numbers, and how to reach parents.

9. Ask for a copy of the discipline procedure policies for your school and read it from cover to cover. There should be steps for what to do when the behavior has moved beyond isolated incidents.

10. Your best plan is to be prepared. Know how you will react in given situations and follow through.

11. If your school does not have a plan for emergencies such as when a student's behavior becomes bizarre or beyond what you are able to handle (this includes fist fights in the classroom), make a plan with a teacher nearby so that you have a code for help. For example, you might cut out an apple and laminate it. When the situation becomes tense, you might ask a student pleasantly to take the apple to Mr. Wilcox next door. We have also used code words such as calling into the office and saying it is Washington's birthday or Betty Boop so that they know there is a problem. If you do not have a phone in your room, ask a student to go to the room next door to tell the teacher a secret word

that you have worked out in advance. The point is to be prepared. It is much easier to stay calm in an emergency if you have a plan and if you have thought out the situations.

A FEW WORDS ABOUT ANGER

Panksepp (1998) identifies anger as "that powerful force we experience as an internal pressure to reach out and strike someone." In this time of great anxiety and stress, we are seeing the lack of impulsivity control more and more from road rage to fist fights. The classroom is no exception. Not only do we see anger acted upon daily, but anger often moves to rage when needs are not met or when the student feels trapped. Given (2002) says, "Rage occurs as a result of being stuck in a fear-flight response when attempts to flee a fearful situation are thwarted." Scientists have found that people with serious aggression usually have low levels of seratonin and high levels of norepinephrine. These chemicals seem to increase the general arousal effects of anger and aggression (Linnoila et al., 1994). Explicitly helping students to examine their concept of themselves may help in lowering this negative behavior. Given (2002) says, "If educators expect students to persevere with learning tasks, then they must attend to how students view themselves within the classroom context." To do this takes patience and consistency. It is a commitment to students and to the community. On every national agenda are the issues of education and the issue of violence in the neighborhoods. As teachers, we have an opportunity to help solve those problems as no other individuals have. Using what we know about the self-system of the brain, we can make changes in our communities that will have long-lasting effects. By teaching students to examine themselves, their motivations, and the picture that they have of themselves, we make the first steps toward change. Given says,

If students frequently act out and are abrasive or belligerent, their own actions become internalized as defining characteristics of self as "difficult." By contrast, if students see themselves as friendly, helpful, and kind, those characteristics become internalized as a definition of self as "pleasant and caring." Students then continue to behave in ways consistent with their self-perception.

WORKING WITH STUDENTS FROM POVERTY

Most of the students who come to us from poverty are not discipline problems. However, there are characteristics that are often attributed to these students that may offer challenges to the student and the teacher. For example, Payne (2001) says that students from generational poverty (poverty for two or more generations) may laugh when disciplined because in their world this is a way to save face. Some other behaviors they may exhibit include:

- *Arguing with the teacher*—Those in poverty often distrust anyone in authority.
- *Inappropriate or vulgar comments*—Inner-city students and students from poverty use a form of language called casual register that includes words from the street.
- *Inability to follow directions*—Procedural memory is often not used in poverty. Students who have grown up in poverty tend to live for now; planning is not part of their day-to-day activities.
- *Fighting*—Fighting is often how children in poverty survive. They do not know negotiating skills because they have not been taught.
- *Hands on others*—Nonverbal data are a part of poverty. The body is important because it is one of the few things they own.

WHAT'S A TEACHER TO DO?

Most schools are run on the ethics, speech, and values of the middle class. In order to work with students from poverty, we must first understand that they may not know the rules of the middle class or why it is important for them to follow those rules. Students need to know that there is one way to be successful on the streets and another way to be successful in school and on the job. Telling students that they must never laugh in the face of fear could get them killed on the streets. We want them to survive both at school and in their neighborhoods. Help them to understand the difference and why they need to know it. Here are some other ideas that may help as you work with these students:

1. Understand the reason for the behavior.

2. Help students to see other options for their behavior while in school.

3. Provide lots of kinesthetic activities. These students will not do well in an environment where they must sit for long periods of time and listen to lecture. (Actually, few of us do well in that setting.)

4. Teach them positive self-talk. These students often come to us believing that they cannot be successful. Demonstrate for them how you use self-talk as you walk through problems. Since they do not have experience with procedures that require step-by-step directions, help them to use self-talk to walk through procedures.

5. Don't argue with the students. Instead, ask them to tell you what they did, why they did it, and another way they could do it next time. You may need to help them with options.

6. Speak to them in the adult voice. Payne (2001) defines this as a voice that is "nonjudgmental, free of negative nonverbal, factual, often in question format, and attitude of win-win." Some questions this voice might use include:
   - In what ways could this be resolved?
   - What are the choices in this situation?

- These are the consequences of that choice.
- We agree to disagree (Payne, 2001, p. 110).

In Conclusion

The four major causes of misbehavior in the classroom include the need for attention, power, revenge, and self-confidence. There are specific activities that can be identified in students that relate to each of the needs. When the needs are not met, the behavior may escalate and become difficult to control. Of the three factors involved in any discipline problem—the teacher, the student who is misbehaving, and the rest of the class—the one we can control is ourselves. It is important that we do not take the behavior personally, that we remain calm, that we take care of the behavior immediately and consistently, and that we deal with it appropriately. The Master Teacher lists seven primary physical needs that affect behavior and eight secondary needs that are physiological. The primary needs include such things as:

1. *Hunger*—Not just immediate hunger but improper nutrition, too much carbohydrate, and inadequate calories for the body to operate at an optimum level.

2. *Thirst*—Our brains need hydration, not just at intervals, but also throughout the day. Inadequate fluid intake has an immediate reaction on the brain and learning. The use of certain drugs can also cause excess thirst in students.

3. *Relationships*—With the teacher, other students, or anyone outside of the classroom may be the underlying cause of misbehavior.

4. *Space and other physical factors*—The classroom itself may be the problem. Inadequate lighting, heat, air, or resources affect behavior.

5. *Rest and breaks from routine*—Even the most interesting of subjects can become boring when the body has

not had adequate rest or breaks in the learning. Provide opportunities for students to talk to one another, to take breaks, and opportunities for think time.

6. *Fear of pain*—Pain can be physical or emotional, and both can inhibit learning. The teacher should be aware of conditions within the classroom that facilitate emotional pain and work to eliminate them.

7. *Need for a restroom break*—Some students are too shy to ask to be excused. Make sure that you have a plan in place for going to the restroom and that the fear that someone might take advantage of the plan does not overshadow providing opportunities for students to leave the room.

When the underlying problem does not fall into any of the seven primary reasons listed above, look to the four motivators of power, attention, revenge, or lack of self-esteem for the underlying cause. Before dealing with the behavior, seek to identify what it is and the possible causes so that you can more effectively deal with it on a permanent basis. Changing behavior is not just a quick fix; it should be an opportunity to help students see their behavior for what it is and to find positive ways to satisfy the need.

Table 3.1 can act as a guide as you identify behaviors in your classroom.

Table 3.1   Identify the Problem Behavior

Revenge	Power	Self-Concept	Attention
Defaces property	Refuses to follow rules	Emotional	Speaks out without permission
Fights or bullies	Criticizes	Will not participate	Gets up without permission
Argues	Bosses other students	Blames others for failure	Class clown
Does things own way	Tries to take over class	Threatens to drop out	Makes noises to entertain

4

Planning That Facilitates Positive Behavior

One of the major reasons often cited for teacher burnout is the lack of discipline in the classroom. Many times I have heard teachers lament that if only they could get their students to pay attention, they could get so much done. This chapter will deal with some of the important tactics that teachers can use to help assure that learning time is maximized in the classroom.

Good planning goes a long way toward creating a classroom environment that facilitates good learning behavior. Even the most creative student needs structure. Students need to know both the perimeters and the expectations of the teacher. In the book on planning, we discuss this function in detail. For the purposes of this book, it is important to note that the teacher needs to think through those planning steps that will help to prevent off-task or disruptive behavior. Burke (1992) says, "The most effective way to handle discipline problems is to prevent them." Students are far more secure when they know what to expect. One of the key roles of the teacher is as manager of the classroom. Being a manager is not the same thing as being a sovereign ruler. Good managers take input from those they manage, and they are careful listeners.

CHARACTERISTICS OF GOOD MANAGERS

McCune, Stephens, and Lowe (1999) say that effective managers use planning and preplanning daily.

> Planning means being prepared each day with lesson plans and everything needed to implement those plans. Preplanning means going through each lesson mentally from the student's point of view and anticipating explanations, information, and directions that they will need in order to carry out the lesson successfully.

Let's look at the characteristics of an effective manager in light of planning for positive student behavior and learning.

1. Effective managers are good leaders. They model the behavior that they expect for their students, and they lead students to understand what is meant by positive behavior. They do not assume that students will come to the classroom with the necessary social and emotional skills to be successful; they weave these skills into the cognitive skills of the classroom. They specifically teach students how to control impulsivity so that tasks are completed even when the student encounters difficulty. They also teach students how to control impulsivity in terms of behavior, especially if the student comes from the inner city. Effective managers teach students how to use positive self-talk to help them work through problems. They demonstrate for students how they use self-talk themselves.

2. Effective managers build resiliency in their students. They do this by:

- Gathering, organizing and interpreting data on their students in regard to test scores, socioeconomic status, and interest levels. They use interest inventories (teacher-made) and information from multiple intelligences to guide them as they make assignments in the classroom.

- Creating a positive relationship with each student. The classroom is not a sea of faces to talk to but is made up of individuals who are unique and who have the need to be accepted. The effective manager will instill in students the belief that it does not matter what they have done in the past; this class is a new beginning. They will also have high expectations for every student regardless of socioeconomic status, race, ethnicity, or gender and will reinforce that belief by the way they treat each student, by their expectations, and through the resources brought into the classroom.

- Providing specific and frequent feedback to each student so that they can monitor and adjust their own work and so that the metacognitive system can function at an optimum level.

- Understanding the differences in students from the inner city, students from poverty, and English language learners. The effective manager does not assume that all of these students will come to the classroom equipped with the speech, rules, and guidelines of the middle class (around which most schools are built).

- Using contextualization in teaching. Inner-city and students from poverty learn from the context of the information. They do not do well with memorizing facts, dates, times, and definitions that have not been taught in the context of what they mean. These students often lack the verbal skills to embed strings of words.

- Using pluralization. Teachers who teach only one way will miss many of the students in the classroom. A teacher who understands pluralization will teach content from a variety of frameworks and to a variety of modalities. For example, the effective manager will use several forms of visual models to help students learn, including linguistic organizers, nonlinguistic organizers, and models.

3. Effective managers are able to multitask and to control behavior problems quickly and quietly. "Effective managers are able to secure the cooperation of students, maintain their involvement in instructional tasks, and attend to the clerical or business duties of the classroom quickly and smoothly" (McCune et al., 1999). For example, in my classroom, my students begin each day in their study groups (assigned at the beginning of school) with a question, task, or problem that I have given them to complete in the first five minutes of class. This provides me with time to check roll, take up work, talk to students who have been absent, and so forth, and maintain an organized flow in the classroom. McCune et al. (1999) say that good managers "in discipline situations, use the least intrusive interventions necessary to stop or redirect inappropriate behavior, ensuring at all times that the dignity of the student, even the seriously disruptive student, is preserved."

4. Effective managers know the correct sequence to use in handling off-task behavior. They will help prevent off-task behavior by using the seven steps discussed in Chapter 2 as a first step. For simple off-task behavior they may use eye contact, moving closer to the student, or facial expressions to bring the student back on-task. For continued off-task behavior, the effective manager may call the student's name and ask a question about the learning or move to the student's desk and quietly speak to the student. More elevated measures are used only when necessary and then the teacher tries to keep

those encounters private. The teacher de-escalates situations by remaining calm, moving slowly to action, and by not taking the behavior personal. Unless the teacher has specifically done something to provoke the student, this type of behavior is rarely personal toward the teacher, though it may seem that it is. These behaviors are often about power and made by students who do not feel empowered. We empower students by giving them choices and by providing face-saving options.

5. Effective managers know that both the emotional and the physical climate are important factors that affect human behavior. We all want to feel accepted in the environments in which we live. If you have ever had the experience of feeling that a teacher or colleague did not accept you, then you know how painful and stressful that can be. We do not thrive in these kinds of circumstances; as a matter of fact, we often shut down completely. Marzano (1992) offers these ideas for helping students feel accepted:

   - Make eye contact with all students. Minority students often complain that their Caucasian teachers do not make eye contact unless they are talking about minority issues.
   - Be sure that you pay attention to all quadrants of the classroom. Move about the room to be sure that no one is neglected.
   - Call all students by their first or preferred name. In my classroom, I conduct activities at the beginning of each semester or year to assure that not only do I know each of my students, but that they know each other. I spent a morning with a member of a gang in my area who talked to me candidly about gangs and about what enticed him to become a member at a young age. One of the remarks that he made to me has had a great impact on what I do in my

classroom. He said, "It is more difficult to harm someone you know." I make sure that no one in my classroom is anonymous.

- Move toward and stay close to learners. Talk to them individually and get to know them.
- Touch them in appropriate ways, such as high-fives, in celebration.
- Students sense acceptance by the teacher in little ways. For example, a teacher's tone of voice and body language are subtle ways that students pick up on the acceptance or lack of acceptance by a teacher. Try some of the following ideas for questioning techniques:
- Provide adequate wait time for students to respond. Try counting to yourself to be sure that you wait long enough and that you are consistent in the amount of time that you give each student. Sometimes when a teacher who doesn't believe a student will be able to answer the question does not provide adequate wait time. The teacher may not be aware of doing this, but the student will knows.
- Provide hints to help students who are having difficulty remembering the answer to oral questions.
- Restate the question in another way if the student seems puzzled by the question.
- Dignify the part of a response that is correct.
- Never belittle a student who does not know the answer.
- Create an atmosphere in your classroom that says it is okay to be wrong, but it is not okay not to try.

Think about a place where you like to be. It might be a favorite fishing place, a library, a bookstore, a golf course, or just a favorite place at home. What are the factors that make it enjoyable to be there? How does it smell, feel, look, sound, and so on? The same is true of classrooms that are pleasant. They look, feel, smell, and sound pleasant. Stand at the door of your classroom so that you see it through your students' eyes as they enter the room. What do they see that is visually appealing? Do you use sounds effectively? The tone of your voice, the tone of voice of the students, and the use of music or other sounds goes a long way to setting the comfort of the classroom.

If you are teaching a unit on a period in time (such as the Revolutionary War), bring in the sounds of the times through music. If you are teaching a unit on nature for elementary students, bring in a CD of bird sounds or other nature sounds for your students to identify. Try fun music when students enter the classroom or when they leave; for example, "I've Had the Time of My Life." A great deal has been written about smells in the classroom. Try using an air freshener or an ionized spray to give the classroom a clean smell. One teacher uses the smell of chocolate in her math classroom and then gives her students a chocolate kiss on test day. She says the scores have come up significantly. Our brain attaches memory to context, thus the chocolate has helped her students to remember the math they learned while smelling chocolate. Lighting is important as well. We often do not have control over the lighting in our classrooms, but if you do have control, the best lighting is a combination of outside (natural light) and high lumens.

6. Effective managers provide a sense of order in the classroom. Not many of us work well in a chaotic system, and the same is true for our students. Most students love surprises and uniqueness in the learning, but they also work better in a classroom where there is a sense of order, where they know that the rules that apply to their work today will be the same rules that apply tomorrow, and where rules are followed consistently and fairly. Order refers to the routines that are used in the classroom to assure that conditions are

conducive for maximum learning. As you plan for your classroom, think about how you will do the following (adapted from Marzano, 1992):

- *Begin class*—How will you get their attention, what procedures are in place to assure that students come into the classroom and begin class on time?
- *Ending class*—How do students know that they are dismissed? Do you provide activities right up to the end of the class time?
- *Interruptions*—What have you directed your students to do when someone from the outside or on the address system interrupts you? What about when students have questions or concerns while you are teaching or while students are working?
- *Instructional procedures*—Do you have procedures in place to assure that students move quietly and quickly when getting into groups? Do students know what to do when you move them into activities? I have several routines that I set up at the beginning of the semester that I have found to be very helpful in getting students into the kinds of grouping situations that I need for the activity. The first one is called Appointments. This activity is for those days when I need students to work in pairs. At the beginning of the semester I give them a picture of a clock. On the clock, I ask them to set up an appointment with a different person for each hour on the clock. When I need them to get into pairs, I simply say, "Get out your appointment clocks and work with your 6 o'clock appointment." One of the nice things about this tool is that I can change the groups if I find that I have groups off task. I simply have them go to another partner. I also set up study groups of three who have the responsibility of helping each other prepare for assessments, checking to see that everyone understands the assignments and for discussions.

- *Grading procedures that are fair and consistent*—Tell students up-front what you expect and then stick to what you have told them. I have always believed that students will do quality work when they know what we mean by quality work. There should be no surprises in grading.

7. Effective managers help students to see the value of the task. The importance of the task value to the self-system of the brain was discussed in Chapter 3. We have survived as a species because we have the capacity to determine what is important to know and what needs to be tossed out. Value of the task is wrapped up in the personal goals and needs of the student. Marzano (1992) says,

   This research strongly implies that if educators expect students to be motivated to succeed at classroom tasks, they must somehow link those tasks to student goals. Some powerful ways of doing this include allowing students to structure tasks around their interests, allowing students to control specific aspects of tasks, and tapping students' natural curiosity.

   To tap into students' natural curiosity, ask "What if" questions prior to the learning or find ways to help students relate to the learning. In reading class, you might ask students, What would they do if they were snowed in overnight at school? This is what happens in the wonderful book *Snowed In at Pokeweed Public School* by John Bianchi.

8. Effective managers help students set personal goals for the learning. In order to follow through with the learning and to prevent students from giving up when there are problems encountered with the learning, you must directly teach goal setting. Students need to see for themselves where they are going with the learning and

what kind of progress is being made. This is controlled by the metacognitive system of the brain. When teaching, tell students the goals for the learning and post them so that students can see them. For young students who do not read, send these goals home to parents and use pictures to show what they are going to accomplish.

Ask students to set personal goals for the learning and provide specific feedback to students on how they are doing in regard to reaching their goals.

Directly teach students techniques for monitoring their own work and for making changes to a plan as needed. This prevents students from "blowing up" because they cannot do the work and from giving up when the work becomes difficult. This must be directly taught to students because most students will not come with this ability. It has been said that one of the ways society judges whether we are "smart" is in our ability to make changes in a plan when it is not working and to persevere. Tell this to your students.

9. Effective teachers minimize stress by assuring that students understand the learning and the procedures before putting them into independent practice. Evertson and Harris (1991) offer the following steps to assure that students understand the structures being introduced:

- Explain by giving a concrete definition of the procedure.
- Provide the reason or rationale for the procedure.
- Demonstrate the procedure.
- Present the task in a step-by-step format.
- Explain and demonstrate cues and who will give the cues.

Burke (1992) identifies a well-managed classroom:

Researchers in the area of classroom management offer the following tips for teachers:

- Proactive teachers help prevent discipline problems.
- Students who are actively involved in the lessons cause fewer behavior problems.
- Teachers who use instructional time efficiently have fewer management problems.

Finally, Burke (1992) adds,

The key to effective procedures is consistency. If a procedure isn't working, discuss it and change it. But if the procedure is necessary and it is on the list, enforce it. The breakdown in classroom management doesn't usually start with a bang—it starts with a whimper!

Research shows that a critical time to establish procedures is during the first few weeks of school. This should be a time when class rules are set, and it should also be a time when students are reminded of the class rules for at least the first week of school. It is also very important at this time that the classroom teacher is consistent in carrying out those rules and procedures so that they are reinforced in the students' minds as important. The first week of school is such a hectic time, and it is so easy to let an off-task behavior slide just one time. The problem is that once a behavior or rule is ignored, students tend to perceive that the rule is not important to the teacher. The key is to have a clear and specific plan for introducing class procedures and to follow up each time.

5

Using Cooperative Learning Skills as a Guide

M arzano (1998) found that using cooperative learning to enhance the self-system of the brain had a profound influence on student learning. For that reason, it is appropriate to examine cooperative learning as a tool for helping students to become self-managed.

WHAT IS COOPERATIVE LEARNING?

Cooperative learning is defined as a teaching strategy that enables students to work collaboratively in structured heterogeneous groups toward a common goal while being held individually accountable. In other words, cooperative learning:

- Has structure
- Is a teaching strategy

- Provides opportunities for students to practice the learning together
- Holds students accountable as individuals
- Uses group structures that reflect the class

If the class is 50% minority and 50% Anglo, the groups should reflect those same percentages.

What cooperative learning *is not:*

It is not new, not a replacement for direct teaching, and not simply putting students in groups. Real cooperative learning has structure and purpose; it is not a free-for-all.

Much has been written about cooperative learning. Some of the books include *Jigsaw* (Slavin, 1983), *Cooperative Learning Resources* (Kagen, 1989), *Cooperative Integrated Reading and Composition* (Madden, Slavin, & Stevens, 1987), *Cooperative Work Groups* (Mandel, 2003), *Group Investigation* (Sharan, 1980), and *Learning Together* (Johnson & Johnson, 1975; Johnson, Johnson, Holubec, & Roy, 1984), *The Teacher's Sourcebook for Cooperative Learning* (Jacobs, Loh, & Power, 2002). According to Whisler and Williams (1990),

All involve the elements of cooperative learning but were developed for differing purposes, including learning specific subject matter, providing a framework for main-streaming students with special needs, memorizing basic facts, providing a classroom management scheme, improving relations among different ethnic and racial groups, promoting higher order thinking, and developing social, collaborative, and cooperative skills.

WHY INCLUDE COOPERATIVE LEARNING SKILLS?

Recent brain research indicates that our brains are social organisms, that we are born hot-wired to be social beings. Our environment may nurture that innate ability or thwart it. Schools that encourage cooperative learning strategies are building on a natural need within us to collaborate. Because students come to us with varying ability to communicate with others, for cooperative learning to be effective in the classroom, it must have structures in place to assure its success.

WHAT DOES COOPERATIVE LEARNING OFFER?

The basic difference between cooperative learning and traditional group learning is that cooperative learning emphasizes interdependence and follows a set of basic structures to ensure its success. There is an underlying belief that "we are in this together" in cooperative learning that is usually not present in simple group work. Teachers who use cooperative learning purposefully build in structures that assure there is true collaboration.

In most classrooms there are three learning settings. The first is competitive. In a competitive setting, the premise is that there will be winners and losers. For example, science fair competitions award ribbons for first place, second place, and so on. This is an example of how competition is used in the classroom.

In this setting, students work against each other to accomplish goals that only a limited number can achieve. Students will succeed only if others fail. This is called negative interdependence.

The second setting is individualistic. In an individualistic setting, the underlying principle is that we compete with ourselves. Students usually are working toward a given criterion like a grade. Students who work hard on a theme are doing individualistic work. They are is working for their own grade or satisfaction.

When individual goals are set in the classroom, whether a student reaches his or her goal is unrelated to the performance of another student. In this setting there is no interdependence because students perceive they are in the learning situation alone and that their success does not depend on or affect the success or failure of others.

The third setting is cooperative learning. In a cooperative learning setting, the underlying principle is that we are in this together. We are helping each other to be successful. In lessons where students work together and help each other attain common goals, positive interdependence exists among students. They perceive that they can more efficiently and effectively reach goals if everyone in the group works toward the same goals.

Classrooms should include all three modes of learning. Classrooms of the past relied heavily on individualistic and competitive strategies and very little on cooperative strategies. With the advent of research on brain compatible learning and on emotional intelligence, the importance of including cooperative learning has come to the forefront.

Nancy Whisler and Judy Williams offer the following examples to express the difference in cooperative and traditional learning groups. They say that traditional learning groups have only one leader, are told to cooperate, and the priority is academic goals. The teacher is in the role of teacher, who intervenes when necessary. On the other hand, cooperative learning groups have shared leadership, their priorities are both academic and social skills, and they practice specific social skills that have been taught.

The teacher's role is to interact with the groups and to provide feedback on how they are doing on both social and academic skills.

TEACHING SOCIAL SKILLS

In cooperative learning, specific social skills are taught and reinforced in the classroom. For example, students might work on the skill of taking turns listening and then responding appropriately. Teachers teach this skill by modeling it, asking students to model it, or by discussing what it means. Next, teachers explain to the students that they will be walking around listening to the groups as they work, and they will

Table 5.1   Skill: Listening

Looks Like	Sounds Like
Eye contact	Agreement words
Head nods	Only one person talking
Leaning in to hear	Comments made back only one at a time
Looking at the speaker	Appropriate comments

be making notes about how the students are doing on both the academic skill and the social skill. Teachers might ask their students to tell them what they will see and hear if students are really using the social skill. The students' answers are placed on a T chart such as the one seen in Table 5.1. The T chart should be displayed in the classroom so that it is visible to everyone. As the teacher walks around the room, he makes notes according to what he hears and sees the students doing in regard to the social and the cognitive work assigned.

At the end of the group time, the teacher tells the students what he observed and discusses the information in light of what the students told him they would do and say.

Teachers who use cooperative learning should have a management tool to help them keep up with the work that the groups are doing and their progress in regard to social skills. In my classroom, social skills are a part of my students' grades. They know this up-front, and parents know it as well. Being able to be emotionally intelligent is just as important to being successful in life as cognitive skills. Goleman (1995) says it may be more important.

Form 5.1 shows an example of how I might keep up with my students' progress in social skills. In the first row I have placed the skills that are important in my classroom; you may choose other skills. The rule of thumb is to begin where your students are in terms of social skills. If your students

Form 5.1   Example of Tracking Social Skills Progress

Class . . . . Dates . . . .

Group Members:

Week	On Time	Quality Work	Listening Skills	Positive Remarks
1				
2				
3				
4				
5				
6				

do not know how to get into groups quietly and quickly, that might be one of the skills you teach. The point is that we will never get our students to important skills such as knowing how to criticize ideas rather than people if they do not know simple listening skills. Begin where they are, and then move your students to more sophisticated skills as they grow socially.

6

A Model for Classroom Management

I n the preceding lessons, we have examined how motivation and behavior are affected by the systems of the brain. We have discussed ways to tap into our natural motivation to learn and how to deal with students whose behavior problems are not related to the learning. We have also looked at the urban learner in light of behavior. You know that it is imperative to have a plan for those days when behavior is an issue and that your body language, as well as what you say and do, are important to diffusing situations. In this lesson, you will build a plan to help you as you monitor and work with students in your classroom. Here is the format for that plan:

CLASSROOM MANAGEMENT PLAN

Teacher Name . . . .

Grade Level or Subject . . . .

Level One Implementation: General Behavior Management

1. What will you do to assure that learners feel accepted in your classroom? List three or more specific ideas you will use.

2. What will you do to assure that your classroom reflects comfort for your students? Specifically, what will you do for lighting, visual effects, smell, and sound effects? How will you arrange your room? What will students see when they walk in the door?

3. How will you assure there is order in your classroom? Provide an example of your class rules or norms and how you came up with these rules. How do you handle tasks such as turning in homework, notes, and the like? How do you begin your class? How do you end class? If you teach elementary students, how do you teach them to line up and to get on the bus in the afternoon?

4. What will you do to help your students see the value of the learning?

5. What will you do to help students set and follow through with personal goals?

6. What structures do you have in place to put students into groups? How do you identify and grade your students' behavior?

7. You were given seven tools for changing off-task behavior. For each of the tools, provide one strategy that you will try with your students.

Level Two Implementation: Disruptive Behavior

8. What will you do when a student is disruptive?

9. What will you do when a student talks back to you?

10. How will you control your impulsivity?

11. Do you have a plan for emergency situations in your classroom? What is your plan?

Vocabulary Summary

At-Risk Students

Students are designated as *at risk* of dropping out of school (without intervention) by individual schools based on criteria that might include the following:

- Students who have failed one or more grades or subjects
- Students from low socioeconomic homes (as defined by the federal guidelines on poverty)
- Students with some handicapping conditions
- Students reading below grade level
- Students working below grade level in other subjects, especially math
- Students who have not mastered the state test for their grade level
- Homeless students
- Migrant students
- Students from abuse or neglect

Behavioral Assessment

Behavior should be a part of the total assessment program in the classroom. You may want to use your grade book for making anecdotal notes about behavior or you may choose to set up a separate notebook for keeping track of student behavior.

Body Language

Body language refers to the nonverbal ways that we communicate. Students pick up on what we do with our expressions, our eyes, our mouths, and our hands as we talk to them. We may be able to smile at a student we do not particularly like but our eyes and our body stance may reveal something entirely different. When faced with discipline problems, it is important that we communicate with our words and also with our body language. The communication should say, "I like you, I do not like your behavior at this time." Students do not want to be talked down to, they do not want someone pointing a finger at them, and they do not want someone demonstrating dislike for them personally.

When confronting a behavior problem, take a few seconds to take two deep breaths and let them out slowly. Turn slowly toward the student. (Fred Jones [2002] says to think of yourself as royalty when you turn. Watch them, they do not make quick, jerky movements, they turn slowly.) We tend to keep our hands above our waist when we are upset. Move your hands loosely to your sides. We tend to stiffen our jaw when angry. Run your tongue over the roof of your mouth to loosen your jaw. Speak softly so that only the student can hear you. Fred Jones suggests putting your palms on the student's desk as you speak. Stay at the desk long enough to see that the student is back at work and then slowly remove your palms from the desk, stand up straight, and walk slowly away. If the student makes a remark as you walk away, stop, turn slowly, and return to the desk. Palms down on the desk and again get the student back to work. Do not take issue with the remark, let it go in one ear and out the other. This is a power struggle for the student. Always take care of off-task and inappropriate behavior. Students know when you ignore poor behavior.

Classroom Management

Classroom management refers to all of the components necessary to assure that there is a sense of order in the classroom, and that the classroom is the kind of place where students learn at an optimum. Management takes a great deal of planning not only for the known but also for the unknown. While teachers plan for the learning, they must also plan for a strong positive emotional base for the learning. This includes:

- The physical environment such as placement of student desks, lighting, the smells and sounds of the classroom, and so on. Desks should be arranged so that the teacher can walk around and between them in order to assist students and to be aware of off-task behavior. Arrangement of the room is changed frequently and when the nature of the learning changes. For example, if students are working in small groups, the desks will be in clusters, or in a T shape if students are working in threes. When students work in pairs, the desks face one another. For large group discussions, a U shape or circle is appropriate.

- The emotional environment includes such things as the tone of voice of both the teacher and the students. There should be a threat-free environment that communicates to students that we are all learners together and that no one knows all of the answers. It also says that it is okay not to know the answer. The important part is to try and to participate actively in the learning. The teacher has high expectations for all students and equips them with the necessary skills to be successful. For example, the teacher recognizes that students may not know how to set personal goals for the learning and thus directly teaches this skill.

- Appropriate measures are taken when students are off task. The measures are consistent and they are dispensed equitably. McCune, Stephen, and Lowe (1999) say, "In general, when dealing with discipline problems teachers should be quick to stop or redirect off-task or inappropriate behavior using the least intrusive means; for instance, dealing with potentially serious disruptions early by using eye contact, moving around the room, or providing short, quiet comments to the disruptive student; and talking privately with students who misbehave to avoid power struggles and face-saving gestures." Jones (2002) says that when training teachers he will often walk around the room and say something to each teacher. After he is finished, he will ask the group if they know to which teacher he issued a reprimand. They usually do not know. This is the way it should be in the classroom. As the teacher, you should be cruising the room while students are working to offer advice, encouragement, and to stop off-task behavior, but it should be done without fanfare or fireworks.

Efficacy

Efficacy is the belief in oneself based on past successes. For example, students who have self-efficacy know that they can learn because they have had experience with success in learning in the past.

Goleman (1995) calls self-efficacy

the belief that one has mastery over the events of one's life and can meet challenges as they come up. Developing a competency of any kind strengthens the sense of self-efficacy, making a person more willing to take risks and seek out more demanding challenges.

Emotion: Positive and Negative

Social and learning situations are often survival encounters. When the brain perceives a situation to be threatening, the stress (fight or flight) response is activated. Nonadrenaline and adrenaline are released, which results in activation of the gut, heart, blood vessels, lungs, skin, sweat and salivary glands, and mobilization of skeletal muscles. Cortisol is released, resulting in suspension of the digestive and immune systems.

Under these conditions emotion is dominant over cognition. The rational/thinking part of the brain is less efficient, and learning is often impeded.

Emotion may impede learning, but it also plays an important role in the enhancement of learning. Any learning that also includes emotion makes the learning stronger. By adding positive emotions to the learning through music, simulations, group activities, role plays, and games, we help our students learn and remember at a more efficient rate.

Emotional Intelligence

Daniel Goleman (1995) is usually associated with the term *emotional intelligence.* Mr. Goleman believes that social and emotional intelligence is essential to success in life and that it sometimes overrides intellectual intelligence. The pieces of being emotionally intelligent include:

1. Being aware of a self-awareness of one's own emotions. This includes not only recognizing the emotions but also identifying the causes. It also means that we know the difference between feelings and actions. We do not act on every emotion.

2. Being able to manage our emotions. This means that we can control our anger and that we do not rely on put-downs and fights to relieve our frustrations and anger. It also means that we develop positive feelings about ourselves and others.

3. Finding positive outlets for emotions. This means that we take responsibility for our behavior and that we act responsibly toward others. We learn to control impulsivity by learning how to monitor and adjust when faced with adversity.

4. Having empathy for others. Emotionally intelligent people can read others' emotions and be sensitive to the feelings of others. They are also good listeners.

5. Knowing how to handle relationships. Emotionally intelligent people can analyze and understand relationships. They are more democratic in dealing with others and have learned to share and cooperate in group settings.

It is interesting to note that these characteristics are built within the metacognitive system of the brain.

Hidden Rules of Society

Ruby Payne (2001) has written a great deal about the hidden rules of socioeconomic classes (poverty, middle class, and wealth). The *hidden rules* are those things that are known by the given group in order to fit into and to survive in the group. These hidden rules affect the way each group looks at various aspects of life, including education. A complete chart of the hidden rules of society may be viewed by visiting the following Web site: www.ahaprocess.com

Impulsivity

Impulsivity is the inability to control one's impulses. Students who exhibit impulsivity react inappropriately to circumstances, and they often give up if things are not going to plan. Students from poverty often come with the rules of the street that emphasize acting on impulse rather than rational thought processes. Impulsivity is controlled in the metacognitive system of the brain.

Learning States

According to Jensen (1997), we all have distinct body-mind moments that alter our frame of mind and body. These states are affected by:

A. "Our thoughts—mental pictures, sounds and feelings; and

B. Our psychology—posture, breathing, gestures, eye patterns, digestion and temperature."

He says that for learning to take place, students must be in the appropriate state. He also says that when we encounter off-task behavior it is often because the learners are not in the appropriate state and that we can change that state. For instance, students who sit at the back of the room with their chairs leaning against the wall and arms folded probably are not in an appropriate learning state. They may feel the learning is boring or not meaningful. We know that before these students pay attention, they need to see the relevance of the learning and to have personal goals for the learning. There are three specific conditions that help keep learners in the appropriate state for learning. They are:

1. High challenge: Not so high that it is frustrating, but high enough to be interesting and to make the student curious.

2. Low stress: This is a state of general relaxation. No stress is boring, high stress is frustrating.

3. Immersed "flow state": This is a state in which students are so involved in the learning that they are not even conscious of it. In order to be in this state, students need to feel challenged and need to have personal goals for the learning.

Modalities

Most of what we learn comes into the brain through the senses. Most of us have a preferred way to learn that involves the modalities through which we receive information. When we are taught in our preferred modality, we are more likely to learn at an optimum level, and we are more likely to believe that we know the information. Studies have shown that students who do not learn the first time probably will not learn until they are taught in their preferred modality. If you have a student in your classroom who does not "get it" the first time, you must change the modality for re-teaching.

Students who seem disinterested in the learning often do not see the meaning or relevance because they are being taught in a modality that is difficult for them. The most common example is students who learn kinesthetically but who are taught in a traditional classroom that relies heavily on lecture. These students are the greatest discipline problem for traditional teachers.

Motivation

Simply stated, *motivation* is the drive to accomplish something. Motivation is controlled by the self-system of the brain. To activate intrinsic motivation (motivation from within rather than for an outside reward), certain needs should be met.

1. We need to see the relevance of what we are trying to accomplish, particularly as it applies to us personally.

2. We need to believe that we can accomplish the task. Self-efficacy is the driving force here.

3. We need a sense of optimism about the goal. According to Goleman (1995), optimism is a predictor of student success and it can be learned. He goes on to say,

Optimism, like hope, means having a strong expectation that, in general, things will turn out all right in life, despite setbacks and frustrations. From the standpoint of emotional intelligence, optimism is an attitude that buffers people against falling into apathy, hopelessness, or depression in the face of tough going.

Inner-city students and those who have grown up in poverty often lack optimism because they have not had much experience with positive emotions. They often believe that they do not control their destiny and that they cannot change what is going to happen to them.

People who are optimistic see a failure as due to something that can be changed so that they can succeed next time around, while pessimists take the blame for failure, ascribing it to some lasting characteristic they are helpless to change. (Goleman, 1995)

Poverty

Poverty is not just about money but about resources as well. The definition of poverty as given by Ruby Payne (2001) is, "The extent to which an individual does without resources." She defines resources as being:

- *Financial*—Money to purchase goods
- *Emotional*—Ability to respond appropriately to situations and having the role models to demonstrate this
- *Mental*—The mental abilities and skills needed in daily life
- *Spiritual*—Belief in a divine purpose and guidance
- *Physical*—Good health
- *Support systems*—Friends and family and backup resources in times of need
- *Role models*—Frequent and appropriate role models who are adults
- *Knowledge of hidden rules*

Generational poverty is defined as poverty over two or more generations.

Temporary poverty is poverty that is temporary and circumstantial, such as loss of job, poor health, or death in the family.

Reward and Punishment

Behavioral psychologists such as B. F. Skinner have had a major impact on behavior modification used in schools in the last century. We know from brain research that the human brain does not work well under a system of reward and punishment and that the reason for off-task behavior is more complicated than first believed.

Self-Management

Students who have good self-management skills have the learned ability to plan for their own learning, to set personal goals, to monitor and adjust those goals, and to follow through.

All of these skills are a part of the metacognitive system of the brain. Students who do not have these skills can be taught self-management by direct instruction in goal setting and in how to control impulsivity. The ability to follow through is one of the ways that our society determines intelligence, and it is critical to personal success.

Structures for Student Learning

Most classrooms use one or more of the following structures:

- *Independent learning*—Students work on the material alone
- *Cooperative learning*—Students practice the learning together
- *Competitive learning*—Students compete with each other for places and grades

An effective classroom will use all three structures as appropriate to the age and learning levels of the students.

The first setting is competitive. In a competitive setting the underlying principle is:

Competitive: I win, you lose. I lose, you win.

In competitive settings students work against each other to accomplish goals that only a limited number can achieve. Students will succeed only if others fail. This is called negative interdependence.

The second setting is individualistic. In an individualistic setting the underlying principle is:

Individualistic: I win, you win or lose. You win, I win or lose.

When individual goals are set in the classroom, whether a student reaches his or her goal is unrelated to the performance of another student. In this setting there is no interdependence because students perceive they are in the learning situation alone and that their success does not depend on or affect the success or failure of others.

The third setting is cooperative learning. In a cooperative learning activity the underlying principle is:

Cooperative: We are in this together. If you win, I win. If you lose, I lose.

In lessons where students work together and help each other attain common goals, positive interdependence exists among students. They perceive that they can more efficiently and effectively reach goals if everyone in the group works toward the same goal.

It is important to note that the purpose of cooperative learning is for students to practice the learning together so that when it comes time to be individually assessed they can be successful. For the purposes of this workshop, teachers should not give group grades (except on the group's ability to work together). Grades are given on individual ability.

Study Groups

This term comes from cooperative learning. *Study groups* usually consist of three or four students who work together for six weeks or longer. If you have a student who is absent a great deal, put an extra student in the group. Study groups work together when it is appropriate to work in small groups. (If you have not used grouping before, start with a small group— never more than three or four until you and your students get used to the process.) The purposes of the study groups include:

1. Studying together

2. Practicing or discussing the learning together

3. Working on activities

4. Peer evaluations

I have my study groups meet at least once a week for a few minutes to see if everyone has their work and if everyone understands the work, the assignments, and the expectations.

Sometimes students don't tell the teacher that they do not understand but will tell the group, and then we can intervene.

I set up my study groups by personality types. For example, I try to put someone in each group who is very traditional, a leader, and will follow through. I try to put someone in each group who is creative, and someone who is a good communicator. I would not put three traditional leaders together because they would argue over who is in charge. I would not put three creative types together because they often have great ideas but do not want to follow through with the details, and I would not put three communicators together because they would be so busy talking they would not get the work done.

I provide activities to help the groups get to know one another and so they will bond. The amount of time that it takes to do this is well worth it because when these groups work well together, we can learn so much more.

Temporary Groups

Temporary groups work together for an activity, and they change frequently. I use a technique called Appointments at the beginning of the semester to set up these groups. I have my students set up 12 appointments for the semester (with 12 different students); on the days I need students to work in pairs, I already have the structure in place.

Thinking Systems

Marzano (2001) identifies three systems in the brain that control our thinking and learning. These systems are important to a study of behavior and management because they relate directly to motivation and the processes of self-management.

All learning begins in the self-system of the brain. This is the system that decides whether we will pay attention and how we feel about the learning in general. The factors that influence this system are:

1. How we view the importance of the learning

2. Self-efficacy

3. How we feel about the learning

4. Our intrinsic motivation to learn

Learning next moves to the metacognitive system, which is influenced by:

1. Our ability to set personal goals

2. Impulsivity

3. Our ability to monitor our own work

4. Our ability to make changes in our plans when we encounter problems with implementation

5. Our ability to follow through

Last, learning moves to the cognitive system, which controls our acquisition and storage of knowledge and procedures.

Verbal Language of Discipline

Payne (2001) talks about the three voices with which we speak to students and they speak to us in discipline situations.

1. The *child voice*, which is defensive, victimized, emotional, strongly negative, and may also be nonverbal. Examples include: Quit picking on me. Don't blame me. He did it.

2. The *parent voice*, which is authorative, directive, judgmental, punitive, from a win-lose mentality, and sometimes threatening. Example includes: You shouldn't do that. You do as I say. That's stupid.

3. The *adult voice*, which is nonjudgmental, free of negative nonverbals, factual, win-win, and often

presented as a question. Examples include: These are the consequences of that choice. We agree to disagree. I would like to recommend. In what ways can this be resolved?

Payne (2001) says that we need to deal with discipline problems in the adult voice, and that we need to provide examples for students for how they should have handled the situation.

Vocabulary
Post-Test

A t the beginning of this book, you were given a vocabulary list and a pre-test on that vocabulary. Below are the post-test and the answer key for the vocabulary assessment.

VOCABULARY POST-TEST

Instructions: Choose the one *best* answer for the questions provided.

1. Self-management skills are regulated by the . . .
   A. Self-system
   B. Metacognitive system
   C. Cognitive system
   D. Regulatory system

2. Efficacy relates to . . .
   A. Past success
   B. The regulatory system
   C. Empathy
   D. Heredity

3. Most students are . . .
   A. Kinesthetic
   B. Auditory
   C. Visual
   D. Olfactory

4. The best structure for the classroom is . . .
   A. Independent learning
   B. Cooperative learning
   C. Competitive learning
   D. A combination of all three structures

5. Which characteristic is not true of temporary groups?
   A. Meet every day
   B. Meet for a short segment of time
   C. Support one another
   D. Incorporate social skills

6. Which of the following characteristics is not an indicator of being at risk?
   A. Economic conditions
   B. Past failure
   C. Reading skills
   D. Single-parent home

7. Hidden rules relate to . . .
   A. Class norms that are not posted.
   B. Schools that do not use rubrics.
   C. Socioeconomic groups
   D. Parents who are uninformed.

8. Having empathy for others is a characteristic of . . .
   A. Emotional intelligence
   B. The cognitive system
   C. Modalities
   D. Impulsivity

9. Intrinsic motivation is . . .
   A. Based on rewards
   B. Controlled in the self-system
   C. Controlled in the cognitive system
   D. Controlled in the metacognitive system

10. Which of the following is true of learning states?
    A. Students need low challenge.
    B. Students need low stress.
    C. Students need no stress.
    D. Students do not need challenge.

11. Which of the following statements is *true* of cooperative learning?
    A. We practice cooperative learning when we put students into groups.
    B. Cooperative learning always includes social skills.
    C. Cooperative learning groups are usually groups of four.
    D. Cooperative learning should be a part of every lesson.

12. Students who quit a project because they have a problem that they cannot solve are demonstrating . . .
    A. Metacognitive problems
    B. Impulsivity
    C. The child voice
    D. Cognitive problems

13. A teacher who has been lecturing in the classroom for 20 minutes decides to put the students into study groups to learn the additional information. This teacher is most probably . . .
    A. At the end of the class time
    B. Introducing the unit
    C. Practicing goal setting
    D. Changing learning states

14. If a teacher has asked the students to practice the learning by building models, which system of the brain is going to be most important in monitoring the learning?
    A. Self
    B. Metacognitive
    C. Cognitive
    D. Experimental

15. When we are angry we should keep our hands . . .
    A. Behind our back
    B. Above our waist
    C. At our sides
    D. Folded

16. Mr. Walters has been cruising his classroom to help students when he notices that a student has turned around in his desk to talk to another student. Mr. Walters walks to the student's desk. What should he do next?
    A. Stare at the student.
    B. Ask the student to step into the hall.
    C. Speak to the student so that everyone can hear.
    D. Put his palms on the student's desk.

17. When Mr. Walters starts to move away from the student's desk, he notices that the student has turned only partially around toward her desk. What does this usually indicate?
    A. The student will go back to talking to her neighbor when Mr. Walters walks away.
    B. The student is not comfortable in the room.
    C. The student feels dejected.
    D. The student is insecure with the situation.

18. Once the student goes back to work, Mr. Walters thanks her for working and then turns to walk away. He hears the student say, "Yeah, like I care." Mr. Walters should . . .
    A. Ignore the student and keep walking.
    B. Send the student to the office.
    C. Go back to the student and get her back on task.
    D. Respond to the comment.

19. When asking oral questions, which is it important that a teacher *not* do?
    A. Provide less wait time for brighter students.
    B. Restate the question when students do not know the answer.
    C. Give credit for partial answers.
    D. Refrain from calling on at-risk students.

20. Which of the following is *not* true of intelligence? Intelligence is . . .
    A. The ability to solve problems that one encounters in real life.
    B. The ability to generate new problems to solve.
    C. The ability to make something or offer a service that is valued within one's culture.

Vocabulary Post-Test Answer Key

1. A	11. B
2. A	12. B
3. C	13. D
4. D	14. B
5. A	15. C
6. D	16. D
7. C	17. A
8. A	18. C
9. B	19. A
10. B	20. D

References

Burke, K. (1992). *What to do with the kid who: Developing cooperation, self-discipline, and responsibility in the classroom.* Palatine, IL: IRI Skylight.

Csikszentmihalyi, M. (1990). *Flow: The psychology of optimal experience.* New York: Harper Perennial, HarperCollins.

Curwin, R. L., & Mendler, A. N. (1988). *Discipline with dignity.* Alexandria, VA: Association for Supervision and Curriculum Development.

Dozier, R. W., Jr. (1998). *Fear itself: The origin and nature of the powerful emotion that shapes our lives and our world.* New York: St. Martin's.

Evertson, C. M., & Harris, A. H. (1992). What we know about managing classrooms. *Educational Leadership, 49*(7), 74–78.

Given, B. (2002). *Teaching to the brain's natural learning systems.* Alexandria, VA: Association for Supervision and Curriculum Development.

Glasser, W. (1986). *Control theory in the classroom.* New York: Harper and Row.

Goleman, D. (1995). *Emotional intelligence: Why it can matter more than IQ.* New York: Bantam Books.

Gough, P. B. (1993). The key to improving schools: An interview with William Glasser. *Phi Delta Kappan, 78*(8), 599.

Jacobs, G. M., & Loh, W. I. (2002). *The teacher's sourcebook for cooperative learning: Practical techniques, basic principals, and frequently asked questions.* Thousand Oaks, CA: Corwin Press.

Jensen, E. (1997). *Completing the puzzle: The brain-compatible approach to learning.* Del Mar, CA: The Brain Store, Inc.

Jensen, E. (1995). *The learning brain.* Del Mar, CA: The Brain Store, Inc.

Johnson, D., & Johnson, R. (1975) *Learning together and alone: Cooperation, competition and individualization.* Englewood Cliffs, NJ: Prentice Hall.

Johnson, D. W., Johnson, R. T., Roy, E., & Holubec, J. (1984). *Circles of learning: Cooperation in the classroom.* Alexandria, VA: Association for Supervision and Curriculum Development.

Jones, F. (2002). Available online at www.fredjones.com

Kagan, S. (1989) *Cooperative learning resources for teachers.* San Juan Capistrano, CA: Resources for Teachers.

Linnoila, M., Virkkunen, M., Scheinin, M., Nuutila, A., Rimon, R., & Goodwin, F. K. (1994). Low cerebrospinal fluid 5-hydroxyindoleacetic acid concentration differentiates impulse from nonimpulsive violent behavior. In R. Masters & M. McGuire (Eds.), *The neurotransmitter revolution: Serotonin, social behavior, and the law* (pp. 62–68). Carbondale: Southern Illinois University Press.

Mandel, S. M. (2003). *Cooperative workgroups: Preparing students for the real world.* Thousand Oaks, CA: Corwin Press.

Marzano, R. J. (1992). *A different kind of classroom: Teaching with dimensions of learning.* Alexandria, VA: Association for Supervision and Curriculum Development.

Marzano, R. J. (1998). *A theory-based meta-analysis of research on instruction.* Aurora, CO: Mid-continent Regional Educational Laboratory (McREL).

Marzano, R. J. (2001). *Designing a new taxonomy of educational objectives.* Thousand Oaks, CA: Corwin Press.

Marzano, R. J., Pickering, D. J., & Pollock, J. E. (2001). *Classroom instruction that works.* Alexandria, VA: Association for Supervision and Curriculum Development.

Master Teacher. (2002). Available online at www.disciplinehelp.com.

McCune, S. L., Stephens, D. E., & Lowe, M. E. (1999). *How to prepare for the ExCET.* Hauppauge, NY: Barron's Educational Services.

Panksepp, J. (1998). *Affective neuroscience: The foundations of human and animal emotions.* New York: Oxford University Press.

Payne, R. K. (2001). *A framework for understanding poverty.* Highlands, TX: Aha! Process Inc.

Sharon, Y., & Sharon, S. (1992). *Group investigation: Expanding cooperative learning.* New York: Teacher's College Press.

Slavin, R. E. (1983). *Cooperative learning.* New York: Longman.

Sprenger, M. (2002). *Becoming a wiz at brain-based teaching: How to make every year your best year.* Thousand Oaks, CA: Corwin Press.

Stevens, R. J., Madden, N. A., Slavin, R. E., & Farnish, A. M. (1987) Cooperative Integrated Reading and composition: Two field experiments. *Reading Research Quarterly, 22,* 433–454.

Tomlinson, C. A. (1999). *The differentiated classroom: Responding to the needs of all learners.* Alexandria, VA: Association for Supervision and Curriculum Development.

Whisler, N., & Williams, J. (1990). *Literature and cooperative learning: Pathway to literacy.* Sacramento, CA: Literature Co-op.

Index

**CORWIN
PRESS**

The Corwin Press logo—a raven striding across an open book—represents the happy union of courage and learning. We are a professional-level publisher of books and journals for K-12 educators, and we are committed to creating and providing resources that embody these qualities. Corwin's motto is "Success for All Learners."